Abandoned, Abused, and Adopted

In the Plan
and Hand of God

An Inspirational True Story of Transformation
Abandoned, Abused, Adopted in the
Plan and Hand of God
An Inspirational True Story of an Overcomer

Dr. Nancy Tillman Franklin B.S., M.S., Ph.D.

PRESS

Acknowledgments

I humbly and graciously dedicate this book to God the Father, God the Son, and God the Holy Spirit. My deepest gratitude flows from my heart and goes out to my husband, Charles Rudolph Franklin Jr., and to my son, Charles Rudolph Franklin III; your unfailing support is truly a treasure to be appreciated throughout eternity.

Thanks also to my extended family, all fivefold ministry leaders, the body of Christ, and the world, through whom the grace and mercy of God have taught me the gift of love. I extend a very special thank you to both Pastor Ricardo H. Jones and Sheryl J. Avery for their administrative work in this project.

My heartfelt prayers go out to the readers of this book. God bless you, and may you be inspired, encouraged, and strengthened, and may you experience the love of God as you journey through the reading of this book.

Contents

Chapter 1
Abandoned by Parents

In the Plan and Hand of God

The journey of abandonment started for me at the tender and all-too-innocent age of three years old. Let me digress just a little. On October 28, 1960, I was born to a mother heavily dependent upon the welfare system and to an alcoholic father who drank so much he could not function unless there was strong liquor running through every inch of his veins.

I was not old enough to attend school, but my mother sent me to school with my older sisters. I ended up in a kindergarten class, where the teacher took me into her class and refused to send me back home. This same teacher ended up adopting me at the tender age of three and later became my first-grade teacher.

This particular morning, as the bus would always pick us up for school, I was the only child out of my parents' eight children that was awakened to get dressed for school. My mother waited with me by the bus stop and watched me get on the bus. I enjoyed going to school so much that the thought to ask my mother why my sisters were not getting on the bus for school never crossed my mind. Without my knowledge, my mother had written a note and carefully placed it in my backpack.

The note from my mother informed the teacher that she needed help, and she went on to ask the teacher to keep me until further notice from her, for she could not care for me. Not knowing this note was in my backpack, I went to school. I placed my backpack in the same place as all the other children; and as far as I know, the teacher never got the note, for at the end of the school day, I was placed on the bus to return home.

When I arrived home, the house was deserted. The door was unlocked, and no one was home. My eyes danced through the house, and I saw no furniture, no clothes, no food; there was only the smell of emptiness. I stayed on the front porch waiting for someone to show up, but seconds turned to minutes and minutes turned to hours. To my surprise, absolutely no one came home.

Not knowing where to go or what to do, I waited and waited. I watched the sun as it slowly conceded to the still, cold nightfall to rule and cover my deserted home in utter darkness. Our house was ten miles from the main road deep in the country woods, with no heat and dilapidated to say the least. Knowing the location and condition of our house, fear began to tug at my heartstrings, yet I refused to cry.

Instead, I courageously grabbed hold of my mustard- seed faith and began to walk on that long, ten-mile dirt road towards the main road in hopes of finding somebody, anybody, that could help me find my family. The silvery moonlight pierced the darkness of the night and shined ever so slight a light along the cold dirt road. I heard the owls, hooting in the dark. I heard the howls of the coyotes and other animals scurrying about in the woods. I was not afraid, because out of all the sounds that were moving through the air, I clearly heard a sweet, gentle voice speaking to me, saying, "I'm here. Keep walking." At that moment in time, little did I know it was the voice of my heavenly Father, God.

I felt such a peace and comfort as I continued to travel down the long, cold dirt road with no civilization in sight. There was nothing but woods and the crackling and shaking sound of leaves as the night

11

wind blew; in fact, the wind felt as if a hand were ushering me to keep moving me forward. Finally I saw an image of a house appearing in the distance. The house I ended up knocking on the door of was the house of my school-bus driver.

This sweet lady, who was a Spirit-filled woman, let me into her home that night. (I was told later on in life that the distance I walked as a child that night was seven miles.) The school bus driver prayed for me and tucked me in for the rest of the night in a warm bed. At daybreak she woke me up, and we rode to school together on that bus I knew so well. Upon arrival the school bus driver turned me over into the hands of my schoolteacher, the very one the note was intended for.

I later learned that my biological parents left the city because staff personnel from the Department of Family and Children Services (DFAC) were threatening to take the children from my mother and place them in foster care. For the first time, the feeling of rejection gently rested upon my shoulders, as reality slapped me in the face: my mother did not want me.

While I was in the care of the schoolteacher, she and others were astonished that I had survived the freezing temperature during the walk that night from my abandoned home to the sweet lady's house.

I knew that it was only the *plan and hand of God* that had completely consumed my frail body and guided me to safety. Looking back now, this would have been something that I would never do or advise anyone that I know to do.

I am convinced that Jeremiah 1:4–5 and 29:11, as found in the Holy Scriptures, apply to each of our lives:

"The word of the Lord came unto me saying, Before I formed thee in the belly, I knew thee; and before thou camest forth out of the womb I sanctified thee, and I ordained thee a prophet unto the nations."

"For I know the thoughts that I think toward you, saith the Lord; thoughts of peace and not of evil, to give you an expected end."

So no matter if you had a rocky start in life on a cold, rugged, dark dirt road, God has an eternally designed plan and a magnificent purpose for your life. No devil in hell can stop God's eternal plan for your life.

God has already calculated everything you thought was a setback, mistake, or stupid decision. Those things do not change God's mind concerning your purpose or your destiny. Romans 8:28 reads, "And we know that all things work together for good to them that love God, to them who are the called according to his purpose." Psalm 37:23 reads, "The steps of a good man are ordered by the Lord, and he delights in his way." So there you have it. Just keep on walking, knowing you are in the *plan and hand of God*.

Chapter 2
Abused by Parents

In the Plan and Hand of God

I have come to learn that the cycle of abuse is no respecter of persons, demographic regions, ethnicity, socioeconomic status, or cultural or religious background that it facilitates itself through. In the 1960s, child abuse just like cellular phones, was not a household item. Essentially, it was unheard of. Generally, you had the community and church having a vested interest in the well-being of children and families. Educators and clergymen were well respected and called upon in the community for various helpful reasons.

I suffered neglect and emotional abuse at the hands of my biological parents. I lived a replay of such abuse again and again at the hands of a foster daughter who was allowed to be a part of my adopted family. In my biological family, the abuse started while I was in my mother's womb. My mother was a diabetic, frail and malnourished due to the fact that every source of income she received to care for herself while carrying me and her other daughters in the womb was taken by our alcoholic father to feed his addiction. My father would drink from sunup to sundown, leaving us with no food, nothing but corn syrup and water from the faucet. That became my daily diet for the three years I was with my biological parents.

This was another example of how God's plan and hand was on my life. Isaiah 43:20 declares that "the beast of the field shall honor me, the dragons and the owls; because I give waters in the wilderness, and rivers in the desert, to give drink to my people, my chosen." Lack of adequate food and clothing left me impoverished and malnourished. My appearance as a three-year-old was stunted in growth, sores all over my head, and worms in my stomach; in essence, I was an extremely sick little girl. I was subjected to living in a house that was unsanitary, and substandard living was the norm. In its dedicatedly poor state, it was still my home.

I had to share a bed, which consisted of a mattress with no box springs placed on the floor, with four other siblings much bigger and older than

I. Oftentimes the weight of the other girls in the bed would crush against me so hard I could barely breathe as they fell into the dead man's sleep. I dared not cry or try to move, for fear of what my parents might do to me if I complained. At three years old, every night I went to bed I prayed the Lord to keep my soul.

Our house was extremely cold at night. There was no heat in the wintertime, and we had wooden floors with cracks and splinters all through the house. Many times I had to painfully pick splinters out of my own feet, and again I dared not cry.

We were sent to school daily with dirty one-piece clothing. My schoolteacher would buy me clothes and re-dress me when I got to school. Many nights were restless due to hearing the arguments and threats hurled at my mother by my father in his drunken state. Looking back, I can clearly see that was another reason why I dared not complain about sleeping on an overcrowded mattress.

Psalm 66:12 says, "Thou hast caused men to ride over our heads; we went through fire and through water; but thou brought us out into a wealthy place."

I always looked forward to school because it was my way of escaping from a dismal situation that seemed to have no end. Going to school, I knew that when I got there, my teacher would always open up class with devotions, which consisted of a song and prayer. It was during those times that I really felt close to an energetically positive force larger than life. After devotions I would always feel a peace, and no matter what happened when I left school, I knew that I would make it.

A true peace that surpassed all human understanding softly rested upon my heart. My teacher's allowing us to sing songs and pray in school created a safe haven and a learning environment second to none.

In the midst of all these treacherous circumstances, I fell in love with my teacher and the prayers she would say every morning over the students. Little did I know that this was God's original design of a lifestyle of prayer that would engulf me forever. Outside of God the Creator, who would have known that this three-year-old girl's (and even to this day as an adult) most precious moments were spent in prayer? God's Word says to pray without ceasing. Philippians 4:6 declares, "Be careful for nothing; but in everything by prayer and supplication with thanksgiving let your request be made known unto God." Philippians 5:16 says, "The effectual fervent prayers of the righteous man availeth much."

Later I would learn that my schoolteacher, my adopted mother, was a Spirit-filled prayer warrior and intercessor who could move spiritual mountains. What a divine setup by God! Through this experience, I fell in love with prayer and would go home daily and repeat the words of prayer I gained and learned through devotions.

I found that God, the supreme Spirit, the Creator of the universe, would talk back to me as I talked to Him. I developed such a dialog with God that it became my means of survival through all the abuse I endured from my parents.

Many people make prayer such a complicated formality, but I found it to be a joy and a treat. When I arrived home, to be able to talk to God was empowering, for He was all I had to survive.

God began grooming me by burning a passion for prayer into my heart at the age of three. He began shaping and molding my spirit for the ministry of intercession and the value of being a spiritual watchman. This is one of the most powerful ministries that exist. Jesus Himself has this job. Isaiah 59:16 reads, "And I saw that there was no man, and wondered that there was no intercessor: therefore his arm brought salvation unto him; and righteousness, it sustained him."

Unknown to my schoolteacher, who adopted me towards the latter part of my third year, I was experiencing abuse in her home—not by her, but by another lady who also lived in the home. This lady was never adopted but was fostered by my adopted mother and sent off to college. She commuted to college, and when I entered the house in which she and my adopted mother lived, the spirit of jealousy crept in unaware and manifested itself through painful beatings I would receive from this woman.

I later found out she had always wanted to be adopted, but instead, she was fostered into the family *(The silently unspoken nuance of one being adopted is that one is chosen and wanted. The undertone of one being fostered is of being taken care of, not really knowing if one is wanted by anyone)*. Not only did I suffer painful beatings out of jealousy, but during the times of my adopted mother's absence, this woman also took me to witch doctors and forced me to drink bitter liquid concoctions intended to do me harm, which she would ironically call "tonics for my health" (Mark 16:18: "They shall take up serpents; and if they drink any deadly thing, it shall not hurt them.").

At the time while I going through each family and suffering abuse, I was in survival mode from the unthinkable to the unimaginable. The horrific occurrences took on a normalcy, and as a child with no point of reference, this was all I knew.

There was no speaking against the abuses that I was undergoing. Speaking out was unheard of, and it was also muzzled by an adult slave mentality coupled with black pride; muffled was the outcry deep within my soul. But through it all, even as a child, I always had this love factor from God and always found refuge in prayer.

I would pray for everyone, my biological as well as my adopted families. I unexplainably loved them so much that what was going on in and around my life never magnified in my mind as something immoral. Early in life, I came to understand the applicable meaning of Proverbs 10:12: "Hatred stirs up strife; but love covers all sin." Matthew 5:10 says, "Blessed are you, when men shall revile you, and persecute you, and shall say all manner of evil against you falsely, for my sake." Matthew 5:44 says, "But I say unto you, Love your enemies, bless them that curse you, do good to them that hate you, and *pray* for them which despitefully use you, and persecute you" (emphasis added).

Truly the plan and hand of God once again was exemplified in my life, because today I love to pray, talk to God, and spend countless hours communing in the presence of the Lord our God. I call God my "daddy," and I know firsthand as Philippians 4:19 says, "But my God shall supply all your need according to his riches in glory by Christ Jesus." I began my spiritual as well as natural journey by leaning and depending on my spiritual daddy to supply my emotional and physical needs, not knowing that as He met my spiritual needs, all other needs in my life were being met also.

As a young woman in the Lord, my passion for God grew stronger and stronger. A press in my spirit and stillness in my heart were ever present, encouraging me and saying, "Daughter, in all you do, let your best shine through." I knew I was not like the other young girls in my high school or college. Being on the cheerleading squad or running with the most popular sorority was not what God wanted out of my life. A thirst for wisdom, knowledge, and praying for others permeated my being. I knew my heavenly daddy wanted me to gain understanding in all my getting.

My earthly family and schoolmates did not understand me, but my God, my daddy, not only understood me, but He also knew me. In knowing that God knew me, I began to trust Him more and more. Oh, how sweet it is to have a strong reliance in God the Father for all things in heaven and on earth! I grew up knowing God loves me.

Chapter 3
Abused by Spouse

In the Plan and Hand of God

When you stand before God and recite your wedding vows, you never think that abuse will come from the very someone from whose rib you were taken. Genesis 2:21–23 states, "And the Lord God caused a deep sleep to fall upon Adam, and he slept; and he took one of his ribs and closed up the flesh instead thereof; and the rib, which the Lord God had taken from man, made he a woman, and brought her unto the man. And Adam said, This is now bone of my bones, and flesh of my flesh: she shall be called Woman, because she was taken out of Man." I, the woman, was taken from a man's rib. As 1 Corinthians 11:7 declares, "For a man indeed ought not to cover his head, forasmuch as he is the image and glory of God; but the woman is the glory of the man."

24

At that time in my marriage, I never initially knew abuse to be abuse because I had experienced my biological father's raging in the house with my mother. This was normal for me. Through numerous dialogs with God and after completing various counseling classes during my undergraduate and graduate studies, I discovered there was an excellent way of communicating with your spouse other than by participating in angry rage wars.

As always I would talk to God, my daddy, and would find the peace to endure the storm. In reading the Bible, in Psalm 107, I saw that God makes the storm calm, so the waves therefore grow still. Before long I began to recognize similarities and connect the dots from abuse through childhood into adulthood. I began to see that anger, hurt, resentment, power struggles, manipulations, and control in the most degrading form had crossed over and followed me into my adult life.

The words *love covers a multitude of sin* are so true because it was only the love of God covering me throughout the storms. Through the love that God gives (in the Greek, *agape*, which is translated "unconditional love"), I began to develop within me a character like God through His love. God's love is not merited on what you can do for Him or how flawless you are. John 15:13 declares, "Greater love hath no man than this, that a man lay down his life for his friends." John 15:16–17 says, "Ye have not chosen me, but I have chosen you, and ordained you, that ye shall go and bring forth fruit, and that your fruit should remain: that whatsoever you shall ask of the Father in my name, he may give it to you. These things I command you, that you love one another."

In the Plan and Hand of God

I started implementing and living the love factor characteristic of God. In the midst of living with an abusive spouse, I can truly say the love of God will diffuse any heated situation and bring you to a state of repentance while changing the stony heart of your spouse to a heart of flesh.

God is so phenomenal, so extraordinary in His plan, that He foreknew the ministerial call on my life. I never knew all that was going on in my life and in my marriage, but God knew the experiences in my life were equipping me for the calling in my life, which involves ministering to children and adults. From my experience, I am able to empower children and adults to overcome the vicious cycle of abuse, moving from a mentality of being a victim to walking in the life of a victor.⌐

Philippians 2:5 states, "Let this mind be in you which was also in Christ Jesus." Had I not taken on the mind-set of Christ Jesus, I would have missed another unique opportunity to minister the gospel of Jesus Christ to not only my biological and adopted families, but to my spouse and his family as well. Psalm 68:6 states, "God sets the solitary in families: he brings out those which are bound with chains." Through marriage, God allowed my seed to come forth, which will do exploits in the sense of heroic acts for the kingdom of God.

I can say with blessed assurance that only God's love can break the cycle of abuse, put the enemy to flight, and allow purpose to be accomplished in our lives. We must always remember that the things God allows us to experience are never just for us alone, but to also assist someone to become an overcomer in their journey. Life at times presents so many roller-coaster rides that turn you up, down, and all around to the point where you feel like the drop is about to kill you, but hold on to God and know that His plan will allow you to live and enjoy the ride.

I became even more determined that these abusive character traits would diffuse with my generation through the power of prayer and the Word and love of God. The very instant you don't feel loved, you can ask God to come into your heart and demonstrate His power. Romans 10:9 declares, "If thou shalt confess with thy mouth the Lord Jesus, and shall believe in thine heart that God hath raised him from the dead, thou shall be saved." Yes, salvation is in the plan and hand of God. He wills that none would perish, but that all should have everlasting life.

Chapter 4
Abused by Church (Organization)

In the Plan and Hand of God

I have heard on many occasions that the church is supposed to be a healing station, a spiritual hospital for those that have been wounded by the world. This is one of the many reasons I am extremely grateful for the church being there, but every time I checked into the church hospital to carry out my purpose, I would always check out feeling further wounded. It was to the point that I would have to check in with God—Daddy—and allow Him to heal me from the wounds I'd received during my stay in the church—wounds inflicted by church people.

Traveling all over the world with my husband, who was a soldier in the military, I was exposed to various religious denominations. The worst-case scenario came in the year of our Lord 1996 when I entered a church at our last and final military-duty station. All I wanted to do was bless the people of God by loving, serving, teaching, and administering the Word of God. Needless to say, when I went into the church, it seemed the perfect place for me. The more God began to unveil the talents and gifts He had given me for the body of Christ, however, the more I experienced reprisal against me.

Ephesians 4:11–12 proclaims, "And He gave some apostles; and some, prophets; and some, evangelists; and some, pastors and teachers; for the perfecting of the saints, for the work of the ministry, for the edifying of the body of Christ." God had gifted me with the ability to write grants and administrate programs that generate money. I had acquired the experience through my secular career in the educational field and was extremely excited to utilize this acquired talent for the church. I saw a need for children's programs and outreach services to benefit not only the church but also the community at large. But what was intended to be something that I enjoyed creating and doing for the Lord and His people became a monster in disguise. I did not know the devil was attempting to use man to sabotage God's plan.

It all started when I was asked by the pastor at that time to leave my job teaching at the state prison to oversee the church's day-care program. I struggled with this decision, but the pastor told me this was what God wanted in my life. I was convinced he was right, so I obeyed and accepted the position offered by the pastor. Still working at the state prison as an educator, I wrote a pre-kindergarten grant, which was approved without a hitch. The pre-K grant allowed the church to receive funding for the day-care program.

In the Plan and Hand of God

My position as administrator and grant writer made me the responsible agent for a fifty-thousand-dollar grant. The United States government was holding me responsible for managing appropriately the cash-valued grant. Therefore, I felt the need to leave my teaching job at the prison and transition to working full time for the church in order to effectively manage the funding that was being provided for the church's day-care program. This was a great financial sacrifice, for not only was my salary going to be cut in half, but my husband had just retired from the military and his salary was cut in half. Stepping out in faith, I left my state job to work full time for the church.

Second Corinthians 1:20 states, "For all the promises of God in him are yea, and in him Amen, unto the glory of God by us." You can stand on the promises of God. Proverbs 3:5–6 also declares, "Trust in the Lord with all thine heart; and lean not unto thine own understanding. In all thy ways acknowledge him, and he shall direct thy paths." I was compelled to apply to my heart the words of Psalm 118:8: "It is better to trust in the Lord than to put confidence in man." I say this, for when I took the administrative position at the church's day-care facility, the entire program was in the red (indicating a deficit, or liability).

The church's day-care assistant director and I took turns going into our personal financial accounts to withdraw funds to help make payroll for the employees. There were times we would delay and even forfeit our own pay so that employees working at the day care could get their pay. I eventually exhausted my retirement funds to help the program come out of the red; and as if that weren't enough, when God pulled the day care out of the red and a slight profit was being gained, the chief executive officer pulled funds out of the day-care account and used them for other purposes not related to the day-care program.

Knowing the government was holding me responsible for any misappropriation of funds, I decided to
take a stand for what is right.

When I took a stand and spoke out against what
was being done with the funds, the next thing I knew,
I was being falsely accused and kicked off the job, no
longer able to oversee the day-care funding program.
I was moved from running the day care to supposedly
receiving a promotion of assisting the church staff in
the main office. Keep in mind that this "promotion"
came without pay (go figure). I was hurt and disap-
pointed, for the attack came from within the walls of
the church leadership. Knowing God had a calling in
my life, I chose to press on in spite of the adversities.

I knew my calling was administration and teaching; therefore, I proceeded to develop and implement
another government-funded program. The church
leadership was excited and gave me their authori-
zation to use church classrooms. With God's help, I
was able to get funds approved for a children's after-
school tutorial program at the church. This program
allowed me to acquire personnel and staff consisting
of women in need of work through the state welfare
program. In doing this, the program grossed over two
thousand dollars monthly.

One would think, wow, finally I would be able to get a salary after months of working without pay. Well, it didn't happen that way. Still no salary was given to me for the work that I was doing. The demand to keep producing was overwhelming, and the church leadership was never satisfied. No matter what I did, it was never enough nor in their minds warranted any pay. The more money brought in through the programs I created, the more avarice built up in the hearts of leadership. The love of money had gripped the heart of man, and the money had generated so much greed that God finally said, "Nancy, enough is enough!" God began to give me instructions on how to write a resignation letter so as to leave that position, and my assignment was over in that particular church.

In the Plan and Hand of God

I thought this would be an easy transition, but it was definitely not so. When I met with the pastor of the church and professionally released this information, along with my letter of resignation, he kicked me out of the church and spoke curses over my life. There I was—unemployed, exploited, and humiliated. To add insult to injury, he even kicked my child out of the after-school enrichment program I had created at the church through God's help.

However, he never did remove my name from the grant programs, although he no longer wanted me to be part of the church. With my name listed on the prekindergarten grant as the overseer, I had to do the right thing and inform the Pre-Kindergarten Department in the State of Georgia that I was no longer a part of that church and to please remove my name from those grants.

Three months later I got a call from the very same church where I had been kicked out by the pastor. They were being audited and asked if I would come and assist them in passing this mandated audit. I calmly responded to that call with, "You all fired me. I am no longer in that position." There was a silence on the other end of the phone. I proceeded to say to the caller, "When the auditors arrive, they can ask me anything that took place during my tenure of employment with you, and I'll be glad to tell them and you."

Of course I became the devil after that call, for I did not say what the pastor wanted to hear. I did not respond the way he wanted me to respond. I chose to respond the way God wanted me to respond. I spoke with honesty and clarity of heart. What a roller-coaster experience! When I thought the ride was just about to end and I could get off, it seemed as if it were starting all over again.

The next church abuse came right after leaving the church previously mentioned and going to help out for a year in a deliverance ministry. God has gifted me with the ministry of helps, and I knew the calling in my life was greatly needed in the body of Christ. The pastor of the deliverance ministry prayed for God to send help. When I arrived, she told me that I was the answer to her prayers and the prayers of the people within her congregation.

From the start, entering that part of the body of Christ, God allowed me to establish a tutorial-enrichment program and food pantry for that church. I was placed over the pastor's aide and faithfully served the people and the leaders within the church. In fact, I served the pastors, for in that deliverance ministry there was a pastor and a co-pastor. I served them both to such an extent that after a year God told me, "Nancy, you have crossed the line. I know you love people, but when you start serving man so that it consumes your time from Me, one has to go; for you will love one and hate the other."

Joshua 24:15 says, "Choose you this day whom you will serve." When I chose God, I began to be treated as an outcast and was labeled a witch sent to devour the church. Through the eyes of God, I was able to see that the deliverance ministry was in need of God's deliverance. God had me to exit the assignment by informing the pastor and letting her know that the real witch was in her inner circle and would divide the very church in which God had placed her as pastor; and she would see the truth. Two months after I left that ministry, what I said to the pastor was exactly what happened, and the one who accused me of being a witch divided the church by starting her own church.

Luke 22:25 declares, "The kings of the Gentiles exercise lordship over them; and they that exercise authority upon them are called benefactors." I feel as if I could write an entire book on church abuse, and probably will, for these are just a few examples of the cases of church abuse I encountered along the journey to the kingdom of heaven.

I have experienced everything from being cursed out in the church, physically jumped on, and negatively preached about as though I were not sitting in the congregation to hear the nasty things being said about me in the pulpit. I have gone from being manipulated to being kicked out of the church, and not a mumbling word did I utter other than "Yes, Lord."

All this was necessary for the apostolic anointing and call on my life. As James 1:2–4 reads, "My brethren, count it all joy when ye fall into divers temptations: Knowing this, that the trying of your faith worketh patience. But let patience have her perfect work, that ye may be perfect and entire, wanting nothing."

Now I am aware of the different Jezebel spirits in the earthly church that operate to silence the prophetic voice of God in the church. Second Chronicles 20:20 says, "And they rose early in the morning, and went forth into the wilderness of Tekoa: and as they went forth, Jehoshaphat stood and said, Hear me, O Judah, and ye inhabitants of Jerusalem; Believe in the Lord your God, so shall ye be established; believe his prophets, so shall ye prosper." Second Chronicles 36:16 goes on to say, "But they mocked the messengers of God, and despised his words, and misused his prophets, until the wrath of the Lord arose against his people, till there was no remedy." Leaders operating under the influence of the Jezebel spirit will be held accountable. Revelation 2:20 says, "Notwithstanding I have a few things against thee, because thou sufferest that woman Jezebel, which calleth herself a prophetess, to teach and to seduce my servants to commit fornication, and to eat things sacrificed unto idols."

Chapter 5
Adopted by Family

In the Plan and Hand of God

*And he answered them, saying, Who is my
mother, or my brethren? And he looked round
about on them which sat about him, and said,
Behold my mother and my brethren! For
whosoever shall do the will of God, the same
is my brother, and my sister, and mother.*
— Mark 3:33–35, KJV

As I stated earlier, I was placed in the hands
of my schoolteacher at the age of three years
old. My schoolteacher adopted me, for my biological
parents had abandoned me as they left the city and
never returned. However, my parents never signed
any paperwork to legalize the adoption.

At the age of sixteen, I went to the Social Security
office to acquire my Social Security number in order

to seek employment, not knowing that such a simple act would force me into the family court system in an attempt to legalize my adoption. Because I was of age, the honorable judge allowed me to decide my fate in choosing who I wanted to be my parents. In my selection, the only parents I knew were my adopted parents, so quite naturally I chose them. As a result of this, friction was created between my biological father and me. He no longer wanted any contact with me and would not allow me on his property.

Twelve years later my biological mother was stricken with cancer, and I would drive sixty miles daily to assist my sister with her care. During this time, she gave her life to the Lord, and three weeks later she transitioned to heaven to be with the Lord.

Two years later my biological father became severely ill and was hospitalized in an intensive-care unit. The day I went to see him, he had just been released from intensive care. I went in with two other intercessors and prayed with him. He gave his life to the Lord at that moment, and then he went to sleep. When I arrived home that night, I received the call that he had transitioned to heaven to be with the Lord. At that moment, I began to praise God, for God Himself had ordered my steps. The very man that God had used to bring me into this world, the man who had abandoned me and later rejected me, was forgiven by me; and I, of all people, was chosen to do his eulogy.

I ended up eulogizing my father. It was an awesome time of spiritual healing and family restoration. Two of my biological sisters, who lived twenty hours away, and whom I had seen only once in my life, attended our father's funeral service. My other two sisters lived ten hours away, and I got a chance to reunite with them. Since then, one of my sisters has moved thirty miles from me, and the others desire to relocate also, thereby closing the physical distance between us.

The sister who moved closer and my sisters who reside in my hometown have all been a wonderful blessing in my life. Each week we check in with one another and have a fun day eating at a local restaurant and shopping at various flea markets. This has also pulled our children closer together. A new generation has sprung forth to birth generational blessings for our family. Our nieces enjoy being with us and often plan trips to bring the family together.

My sisters always look to me as the spiritual advisor. However, they are awesomely anointed in their callings. Each of us has unique giftings and talents placed in our hands from God, our daddy. My sisters have the gifts of sewing, decorating, making baskets and elaborate arrangements, and many other skilled trades. We have established a workday in my sister's shop where we let our collaborative, creative juices flow. I am always amazed at the results produced when the Lord brings us together.

My sister's shop is always a place of ministry. The minute someone passes her house and sees our cars, they know one thing for sure: we are having church. They know we are in there praying, singing, and feeding someone. The passersby usually stop and become partakers, leaving my sister's shop better than when they came in. The Spirit of the Lord is always present at every gathering, and His Spirit ministers to the hearts of all who are there.

In the Plan and Hand of God

Peter therefore was kept in prison: but prayer was made without ceasing of the church unto God for him. . . . And behold, the angel of the Lord came upon him, and a light shined in the prison: and he smote Peter on the side, and raised him up, saying, Arise up quickly. And his chains fell off from his hands. . . . And

*when he had considered the thing, he came to
the house of Mary the mother of John, whose
surname was Mark; where many were gath-
ered together praying. And as Peter knocked
at the door of the gate, a damsel came to
hearken, named Rhoda. And when she knew
Peter's voice, she opened not the gate for
gladness, but ran in, and told how Peter
stood before the gate.*

—Acts 12:5, 7, 12–14

God used my adopted mother to lay a foundation
of prayer and ministry. Then He used my biological
mother for the implementation of ministerial service.
I feel extremely blessed by God to have had two
mothers in my life when there are so many children
and young women whose mothers died in childbear-
ing, suffer grave illnesses, or are strung out on illegal
drugs (crack, cocaine, alcohol, crystal meth, etc.).
However, this is such a unique opportunity to apply
prayer to each circumstance.

In the Plan and Hand of God

Even though mother or father may forsake you,
know that the Word of God is true. Psalm 27: 10

says, "When my father and my mother forsake me, then the Lord will take me up."

Now I've traveled from city to city, gathering people in hotels and resorts or homes to have a prayer experience that's life changing. For me prayer is my lifestyle. I cannot separate my life from ministry; this is the will of God concerning me. This is who I am. I desire to see people have a passion and a love for God wherein prayer (talking to God) is just like dating Him, developing an eternal courtship with Him and having a divine connection that brings the will of the Father from the heavenly realm to the earthly to embrace them like no other.

Chapter 6
Adopted by God

In the Plan and Hand of God

Ye have not chosen me, but I have chosen you, and ordained you, that ye should go and bring forth fruit, and that your fruit should remain: that whatsoever ye shall ask of the Father in my name, he may give it you.

— John 15:16

For as many as are led by the Spirit of God, they are the sons of God. For ye have not received the spirit of bondage again to fear: but ye have received the Spirit of adoption, whereby we cry Abba, Father.

The Spirit itself beareth witness with our spirit, that we are the children of God: And if children, then heirs: heirs of God, and joint-heirs

with Christ; if so be that we suffer with him, that we may also be glorified together. For I reckon that the sufferings of this present time are not worthy to be compared with the glory which shall be revealed in us. For the earnest expectation of the creature waiteth for the manifestation of the sons of God.
—Romans 8:14–19

I feel extremely blessed that I have been adopted twice (double portion). I have been adopted naturally and spiritually. I've gone through earthly adoption proceedings, and I've gone through heavenly adoption proceedings. The benefits of God's adoption are unthinkable, unimaginable, unscripted, priceless, and unforgettable; in essence, an embodiment out of this world. No attorney fees are needed, and there is no need for man's approval or an earthly judge's official seal.

When we tap into God's plan and purpose for our lives, we will see that He is our Father and we are His children. He will never leave us nor forsake us. He wants to take an active role in our lives, if we will only allow Him. The river of joy, peace, and happiness will then flow in our souls.

All that we go through in life is for our making and can be used to make this world a better place as we allow God to operate in our lives in every situation and circumstance.

A special thanks to the partakers of this book for allowing God to minister to you and for sowing into the kingdom of God.

To order additional copies of this book, please contact:
Dr. Nancy Tillman Franklin
Foundation Ministries, Inc.
P.O. Box 272
Allenhurst, GA 31301
Or you may call 912-977-0818/369-8533, or e-mail Dr. Tillman at franklin@coastalnow.net or at franklinfoundation@yahoo.com.

Lightning Source UK Ltd.
Milton Keynes UK
UKOW02f1604230117
292701UK00001B/75/P